A CHILD'S BOOK OF PRAYERS

Compiled by

Janet Cookson and Margaret Rogers

Designed and illustrated by

Judith White

TREASURE PRESS

First published in Great Britain in 1970 by
Oxford University Press under the title
Time & Again Prayers

This edition published in 1985 by
Treasure Press
59 Grosvenor Street
London W1

Compilation and Selection © Oxford University Press 1970

ISBN 1 85051 075 X

Printed in Czechoslovakia
50598

Contents

ACKNOWLEDGEMENTS

Blandford Press Ltd., p. 34(a) from *The Junior Teacher's Assembly Book*, ed. D. M. Prescott; Curtis Brown Ltd., pp. 12(a), 12(b), 29(a), 31(a), 33(b), 34(b), 60(d) from *Children's Prayers from Other Lands*; Church Missionary Society, pp. 15(c), 46(a), 63(b), 68(c), 72(a) from *All Our Days*, ed. Irene Taylor and Phyllis Garlick, p. 84(d) from *All Our Friends*; Miss D. Collins and J. M. Dent & Sons Ltd., p. 19(b), *The Donkey* (last verse), G. K. Chesterton, from *The Wild Knight and Other Poems*; Church in Wales Publications, pp. 17(b), 20(b), 21(a), 21(b), 23(b), 24(a) from *Children's Services*; J. M. Dent & Sons Ltd., p. 61(c), Evelyn Underhill (abbreviated from *Immanence*); Daystar Press, p. 61(a) from *Morning by Morning*, M. G. Munro; Duckworth & Co. Ltd., p. 62, Elizabeth Goudge, from *Thanksgiving for the Earth*; Canon H. W. Dobson, pp. 11(d), 36(b), 45(b), 72(d); The Revd. K. Murdoch Dahl, p. 56(a); Epworth Press, pp. 72(b), 72(c) (both), Donald Soper; Executors of the Laurence Housman Estate, p. 87(d) (pub. Jonathan Cape Ltd.) from *The Little Plays of St. Francis*; Faber & Faber Ltd., pp. 18(a), T. S. Eliot, from *Collected Poems (1909–1962)*, 63(c), T. S. Eliot, from *Murder in the Cathedral*; Victor Gollancz Ltd., p. 87(b), Albert Schweitzer, from *God of a Hundred Names*, ed. Greene and Gollancz; Hamish Hamilton Ltd., p. 24(a), Geoffrey Clifton, from *The Junior Hymn Book*; J. T. Hilton, p. 14(b) from *Starting the Day*; Hodder & Stoughton Ltd., pp. 15(a), 15(b), 17(c), 23(a), 28(b), 36(b), 78(d), 84(a) from *Prayers for the Home*, Brenda Holloway; Margaret Kitson, p. 17(a); Longman Group Ltd., pp. 30(e), 51(a), 60(c), 81(a), 84(b) from *An Anthology of Prayers*, A. S. T. Fisher; Macmillan & Co. Ltd., p. 22(a) adapted from Archbishop William Temple; John Murray Ltd., p. 16(a) John Betjeman from *Collected Poems* (alteration by permission of the author); Methuen & Co. Ltd., pp. 70–71, Padraic Colum, from *An Anthology of Modern Verse*, 73(b), John Oxenham, from *The Sacraments*; The National Society, pp. 29(b), M. Ensor, from *Hymns and Songs for Children*, 34(c) from *Growing Up*, V. Bremner, 44(c), 75(a), 84(b) from *Prayer and Praise in the Sunday Kindergarten*, Eleanor Martin, 78(a) from *Worship in the Junior Schools*, Dent and Martin; A. D. Peters & Co., p. 80(d), *The Birds* (last verse), Hilaire Belloc, from *Sonnets and Verse* (pub. G. Duckworth & Co. Ltd.); St. John the Evangelist Trust Assoc. Ltd., p. 13(c); Student Christian Movement, pp. 45(a) from *Children's Praises*, ed. Simpson and Cox, 79(d) from *A Prayer Book for Juniors*, M. Cropper, 87(a), B. A. Leary, from *A Book of Prayers for Schools*; Mrs. Lesbia Scott, pp. 23(c), 36(d), 47(c)–48(c); Miss Mabel Shaw, p. 78(b); The Saint Andrew Press, pp. 12(c), 63(a), 85(a) from *Sunday, Monday . . .*, R. S. Macnicol; The Society of Authors representing the Literary Trustees of Walter de la Mare, p. 86(a) from *Collected Poems*; United Society for the Propagation of the Gospel, p. 69(a); T. H. White, p. 50(a) from *The Sword in the Stone* (pub. Collins & Sons Ltd.); Mrs. Williams, p. 68(a), Charles Williams, from *Walking Song* in *Windows of Night*, 60(a) from *Taliessim through Logres*; Extracts from *The New English Bible New Testament* are reprinted by permission of Oxford and Cambridge University Presses; Extracts from the Authorized Version of the Bible and *The Book of Common Prayer* are Crown copyright and are reproduced by permission.

As many of the prayers contained in this book have been written by the compilers, all requests to reproduce material other than that mentioned in the list given above should be addressed to Oxford University Press, who will advise the applicant of the copyright position.

If, owing to the difficulty of tracing ownership of prayers or through inadvertence, any rights still surviving have not been acknowledged it is hoped that those concerned will forgive the omission.

How to Use this Book

'Praying' is thinking about God, thanking him, and loving him. That is our part of praying and it is the same as God's part. He thinks about us, thanks us, and loves us in return.

When we think about God, we remember how wonderful he is and how wonderful all his works are. This leads us to thank him for all he has made, and for all he has done for us. It also leads us to think about all the other people he has made; those who help us and those whom we can help. God thinks about us too, about all of us and all our needs, and when we have helped other people he will thank us and say 'well done'.

We love God because he loved us enough to send Jesus into the world to show us the way to find him.

Over 450 years ago, there lived an extremely wealthy wool merchant called Anthony Ellis. He wanted to show that he thanked God for all the good fortune he had enjoyed, so he built a beautiful tower to the little church in the village where he lived. On three sides of the tower he put the words THINK AND THANK GOD OF ALL, so that everyone who went past could see them. This happened in the year 1519, and ever since people have been passing by and reading the words, and they have been reminded to thank God for all he does for us. The words are written in the spelling of the time, like this:

THYNKE AND THANKE GOD OF ALL

The tower stands in a village called Great Ponton. Today a busy main road runs near it, and the hundreds of people who drive by in their cars can look up and read the words on the tower. Perhaps your church has a tower like the one at Great Ponton. Some church towers have ordinary clocks on them and

some have a sundial which only can be read when the sun is shining, so that we can watch the sunny hours go by. As we watch, we remember that when it is dark in our own land the sun is shining on the other side of the world.

In this book the prayers are arranged in sections, like chapters in a book, and each section contains prayers to say at a different time of day. You will find that the prayers take you right through the day from waking-up time to bedtime.

Do not forget that, as the world turns slowly round, it is always waking-up time somewhere and always time to go to bed somewhere else. So at all times there are people in the world who are awake and ready to

THINK AND THANK GOD OF ALL

Although the prayers are placed in sections, this does not mean that they cannot be used, many of them, at other times of day. You will find that some of them really do belong to the early morning or to bedtime, but there are others which you might feel one day were exactly what were wanted at mid-day although they are in the section for breakfast-time. To help you to find the kind of prayer you want at any time, look at the back of the book and on page 89 you will find a list of subjects and page numbers which will tell you where to find what you are looking for. The prayers for animals, for instance, are in the 'Breakfast-time' section, because you may have to feed your pet before or after breakfast; but you might easily feel that you wanted to pray for your pet at tea-time. If you look for 'animals' in the list on page 89 you will see that the kind of prayers you need are on pages 19 and 37.

Each section starts with a short passage for you to read before choosing the prayers you want to use at that time of day. You will not want to say all the prayers every day, of course, but make a selection according to how you feel at the time. Always try to choose a prayer for other people as well as one for yourself.

There are a few poems and short pieces of prose sprinkled among the prayers. They are 'something to think about' before praying, and some pieces have that phrase printed above them.

God is sometimes addressed in the prayers as 'thou' and sometimes as 'you'. In the old days, people said 'thou' to each other, whereas nowadays we say 'you'. Until quite recently 'thou' was always used when talking to God, although it had disappeared from ordinary conversation, but it is now quite common to find 'you' used in prayers. In this book, 'thou' has been kept for the prayers written a long time ago, but 'you' has been used for the more modern prayers. Where an old prayer is rather difficult to understand, an easier version has been printed after it. The two versions are joined by * * * in each case.

The word 'Amen' is usually said at the end of a prayer. It is a Hebrew word meaning 'firmly' or 'may it be so'. It has not been printed after each prayer in this book because its general use is taken for granted.

Some of the prayers are written for saying with other people—perhaps your parents—so they use the words '*we* pray' or 'help *us*'. When you say them by yourself you can change 'we' to 'I' and 'us' to 'me' if you want to. For instance, on page 25 'Dear Lord Jesus, *we* shall have this day only once' could be '*I* shall have this day only once' and on page 30 'O Heavenly Father, send into *our* hearts' could be 'send into *my* heart'.

Remember, 'praying' is
THINKING about God,
THANKING him
and LOVING him.
God does the same for us.

THE LORD'S PRAYER

Our Father, who art in heaven,
hallowed be thy name;
thy kingdom come;
thy will be done;
on earth as it is in heaven.
Give us this day our daily bread.
And forgive us our trespasses,
as we forgive those who trespass against us.
And lead us not into temptation;
but deliver us from evil.

I Waking to a New Day

O God, my Guardian,
Stay always with me.
In the morning, in the evening,
By day, or by night,
Always be my helper.

This prayer comes from Poland.

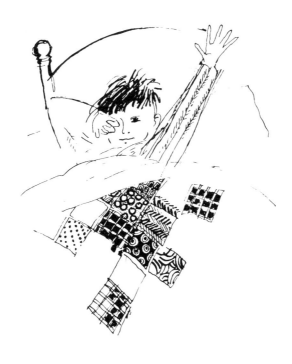

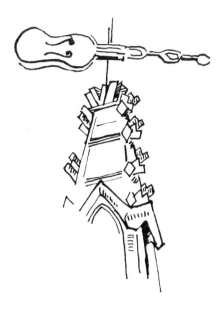

On the top of the church tower at Great Ponton there is something which can be seen on most church towers; a weather-vane. Weather-vanes are pointers which show from which direction the wind is blowing. Sometimes they are shaped like cocks (and then they are called weather-cocks), but the one at Great Ponton is unusual because it is shaped like an old stringed instrument called a viol.

When you wake, you probably wonder straight away what kind of day it is. The weather depends a great deal on the way the wind is blowing, a cold north wind bringing snow, for example. Our thoughts turn to the weather like a weather-vane turns to the wind, and in this section there are some prayers about the weather and the seasons. You are a kind of weather-vane yourself; are you going to point to fair weather today? If it is a special day, like a birthday or Christmas Day, you will think of that too. Every day, thank God for all he does for you and ask for his help all through the day.

This is the day which the Lord hath made; we will rejoice and be glad in it.

My Father, for another night
Of quiet sleep and rest,
For all the joy of morning light,
Your Holy Name be blest.

I will magnify thee, O God, my King: and I will praise thy
    name for ever and ever.
Every day will I give thanks unto thee: and praise thy name
    for ever and ever.

May we show forth thy praise,
Not only with out lips, but in our lives.

SUNDAY

SOMETHING TO THINK ABOUT

Early on the Sunday morning, while it was still dark, Mary of Magdala came to the tomb. She saw that the stone had been moved away from the entrance, and ran to Simon Peter and the other disciple, the one whom Jesus loved.

The stone was rolled away.
There is no barrier between us and Jesus. He is risen.
He is with us always.

We can enjoy his presence and his love; and we go to God's house on Sundays to remember him specially on his special day.

> Ever since that happy morning
> Easter makes our Sundays shine.
> Jesus, help us to remember
> As we keep this day of thine.

O Almighty God, we thank you for this holy day which you have given us for worship and rest. Grant that we may remember to keep it holy, and help us to feel that it is the best day in all the week. Teach many more people to love and honour your day that they, with us, may rejoice and be glad in it, through Jesus Christ, our Lord.

FOR BIRTHDAYS

O Loving God, today is my birthday.
For your care from the day I was born until today,
And for your love, I thank you.
Help me to be strong and healthy,
And to show love for others, as Jesus did.

This prayer comes from Japan.

My Father, all last year you took care of me and now you have
given me a birthday. I thank you for all your goodness and
kindness to me. You have given me loving parents, a home,
gifts, and clothes. Thank you, God. Help me to be a better
child in my new year, to grow strong, to study well, to work
happily.

This prayer comes from India.

Dear Father in Heaven, bless . . . . today very specially
on (*his/her*) birthday. May we and all our family and our
friends be glad today.

The Seasons

Praise the Lord for all the seasons,
Praise him for the gentle spring,
Praise the Lord for glorious summer,
Birds and beasts and everything.

Praise the Lord who sends the harvest,
Praise him for the winter snows;
Praise the Lord, all you who love him,
Praise him, for all things he knows.

NEW YEAR

O my God, I offer you this new year
Which you in love have given me.
Mark it with your Son's own Name.
Help me to live each day worthily.

SPRING

For flowers that bloom about our feet;
For tender grass, so fresh, so sweet;
For song of bird, and hum of bee;
For all things fair we hear or see,
Father in Heaven, we thank thee!

For flow of stream and blue of sky;
For pleasant shade of branches high;
For fragrant air and cooling breeze;
For beauty of the leafy trees,
Father in Heaven, we thank thee!

SUMMER

We thank you, O Loving Father, for the joys that summer brings; for warm days and soft breezes, for the trees and the flowers. Help us to remember that all lovely things come from you.

AUTUMN AND HARVEST

I praise you, God, for all the joys of autumn:
For ripe fruit in our gardens and in our homes;
For the bright colours of the autumn leaves;
For golden corn, and scarlet berries;
Thank you, God.

WINTER

Heavenly Father, thank you for the joys of winter:
For snow and wind, and sparkling frost;
For cosy fires and indoor games;
For warm clothes, and the shelter of our homes on stormy
     nights;
Thank you, Heavenly Father.

O God my Father in Heaven,
    thank you for clear frosty days.
Help me to remember
    old people who are afraid of slipping on the frosty roads;
    the birds who have no water to drink when puddles are
    frozen.
Teach me to help all those who do not enjoy frosty weather
    as much as I do.

The Christian Year

ADVENT

SOMETHING TO THINK ABOUT

The God who created the Heavens
And the wide green marsh as well
Who sings in the sky with the skylark
Who calls in the evening bell,
Is God who prepared His coming
With fruit of the earth for His food
With stone for building His churches
And trees for making his rood.*

This is an old word for the Cross on which Jesus was crucified.

God, who prepared for the coming of Jesus, for his life and death on earth, and for his Church to carry on his work after his ascension, help me this Advent to remember how Jesus was born on Christmas Day, and to make my heart ready for him.

O come to my heart, Lord Jesus;
There is room in my heart for thee.

CHRISTMAS

Heavenly Father,
Help us to remember that Christmas is the birthday of your
 Son, Jesus.
Help us to welcome him gladly and to make room for him in
 our hearts.
Help us to share our happiness with others that we may all
 be more truly your children.
We ask it for your Name's sake.

O Loving Father, we thank you for all the joy of Christmas;
we thank you for the Lord Jesus, who came to earth to save
us; help us to follow him day by day, that we may love him
more, and serve him better; for his dear sake.

Thank you, God, for the joys of Christmas:
For the fun of opening Christmas stockings;
For Christmas trees with twinkling lights;
For exciting parties;
For Christmas cakes and puddings;
 Thank you, God.
Thank you for all the happiness of Christmas-time;
Thank you for the lovely presents we receive;
Thank you most of all that Jesus was born as a Baby on the
 first Christmas Day.
 Thank you, God.

17

EPIPHANY

SOMETHING TO THINK ABOUT

The Magi* came through the snows of winter to find Jesus in
the stable.

> 'A cold coming we had of it,
> Just the worst time of the year
> For a journey, and such a long journey:
> The ways deep and the weather sharp,
> The very dead of winter.'

Years later one said:

> 'All this was a long time ago, I remember,
> And I would do it again . . .'

It is worth an effort to find Jesus.

Lord, show us the Way.

* *The Wise Men*

LENT

Jesus, who spent forty days and forty nights in the wilderness to get ready for the work you had to do, help us to spend part of our day thinking about you, and getting ready for our own work.

PALM SUNDAY

The donkey said:

> '. . . I also had my hour,
> One far fierce hour and sweet;
> There was a shout about my ears
> And palms before my feet.'

This is from a poem about the donkey on whose back Jesus rode into Jerusalem. The donkey was happy to carry Jesus into Jerusalem on that first Palm Sunday. If you look at the back of a donkey you will see a dark mark in the form of a cross in his hair. An old story tells us that it was put there for us to remember the donkey's hour of glory.

Jesus, who rode into Jerusalem on a donkey on the first Palm Sunday, help me to be happy to do work for you.

GOOD FRIDAY

O Saviour of the world, who by thy Cross and precious Blood hast redeemed us; save us, and help us, we humbly beseech thee, O Lord.

* * *

Jesus, who died on the Cross, save and help us all.

Lord Jesus, who for love of us suffered and died upon the Cross; help us to remember your great love on this day and to live always for you.

> Thanks be to thee, our Lord Jesus Christ,
> For all the benefits thou hast won for us,
> For all the pains and insults thou hast borne for us.
>   O most merciful Redeemer, Friend and Brother,
>   May we see thee more clearly,
>   Love thee more dearly
>   And follow thee more nearly
>   Day by day,
>   For thine own dear sake.

This was written by St. Richard of Chichester, who lived over 700 years ago.

> Jesus who died for me,
> Help me to live for thee.

EASTER DAY

O Lord Jesus, our King and our God, we thank you and we praise you for this happy Easter Day; we join with the whole world in saying, Christ is risen! Help us to love you, our Friend and Risen Lord, all the days of our life.

O Risen Jesus, bless all your servants everywhere who are telling the good news of your love; may those who do not know you learn the glorious Easter message, until the whole world together shall praise you, its King; who lives and reigns with the Father and the Holy Spirit, one God, world without end.

ASCENSION DAY

Rejoice! The Lord is King!

In the days when Jesus lived on earth, only the people who lived nearby, or who travelled to see him, could speak with him. If he was in Galilee, men could not find him in Jerusalem; if he was in Jerusalem, men could not find him in Galilee. But his Ascension means that he is united with God, and whenever we are in the presence of God, we are with Jesus, and that is always and everywhere.

Christ has no body now on earth but yours,
    no hands but yours, no feet but yours. . . .
Yours are the feet with which he is to go about doing good,
    and yours are the hands with which he is to bless us now.

This was written about 400 years ago by St. Teresa of Avila.

Teach me, my God and King,
In all things thee to see;
And what I do in anything
To do it as for thee!

WHITSUNTIDE

Lord Jesus:
Thank you for sending your loving Spirit into the world at
Whitsuntide;
Teach me to listen to your voice speaking in my heart;
And when I hear it, help me to obey.
O Holy Spirit, help us to follow our Lord Jesus Christ; speak
to us when we are tempted to do wrong; strengthen us to do
right; show us what we should do; through the same Jesus
Christ, our Lord.

TRINITY SUNDAY

Praise be to God, the dear Father who made me:
Praise to his Son, the Lord Jesus who saved me:
Praise to the Spirit, for gifts he doth send me:
Most Holy Trinity, help and defend me.

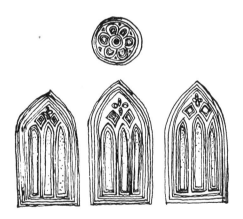

We thank you, Lord, for all the saints and heroes who have fought and conquered in your Name. Fill us with the spirit of adventure and the courage we shall need to follow their example. For Jesus Christ's sake.

ALL SAINTS' DAY

I sing a song of the saints of God,
Patient and brave and true,
Who toiled and fought and lived and died
For the Lord they loved and knew.

They loved their Lord so dear, so dear,
And his love made them strong;
And they followed the right, for Jesus' sake,
The whole of their good lives long.

They didn't live only in ages past;
There are hundreds of thousands still;
The world is bright with the joyful Saints
Who love to do Jesus' will.

You can meet them at school, or in lanes, or at sea,
Or in church, or in trains, or in shops, or at tea,
For the saints of God are just folk like me,
And I mean to be one too.

II Getting Up

Dear Lord Jesus, we shall have this day only once; before it is gone, help us to do all the good we can, so that today is not a wasted day. For your Name's sake.

Getting up is generally a bit of a rush, even if you wake early. A lot of people would say, 'There just isn't time to say prayers.' But God never stops thinking of *us*, and we can think of him whatever we are doing, whether getting out of bed, washing, dressing, going down to breakfast, or seeing that pets are fed.

There is an old story about two men who were talking about praying. They were sure that to pray you must be in a certain position, either kneeling or standing, and that you could not pray in any other way. They were interrupted by another man who told them of an accident he had one day when he fell down a well. 'And', he said, 'the prayingest prayer I ever prayed was standing on my head.' So we can think of God, and thank him and love him, at any time.

Father, we thank you for the night,
And for the pleasant morning light;
For rest and food and loving care,
And all that makes the day so fair.

Help us to do the things we should,
To be to others kind and good;
In all we do at work or play
To grow more loving every day.

Grant, O Heavenly Father, that I may be glad through all this
day:
Glad that you are our Father, and that you love us;
Glad that we can always be sure of your help;
Glad that we can serve you by helping other people.
This is the day that you have made, and I will rejoice and be
glad in it.

May my mouth praise the love of God this morning.
O God, may I do your will this day.
May my ears hear the words of God and obey them.
O God, may I do your will this day.
May my feet follow the footsteps of God this day.
O God, may I do your will this day.

This prayer comes from Japan.

Jesus, may I be like you;
Loving, kind in all I do;
Kind and happy when I play
Close beside you all the day.

O Lord, our Heavenly Father, Almighty and everlasting God, who hast safely brought us to the beginning of this day: defend us in the same with thy mighty power; and grant that this day we fall into no sin, neither run into any kind of danger; but that all our doings may be ordered by thy governance, to do always that is righteous in thy sight; through Jesus Christ our Lord.

* * *

Dear God, who has looked after me through the night, so that I begin the day safely, please look after me through the day so that I may be safe and happy doing what you would like me to do, for Jesus' sake.

Defend, O Lord, this thy servant with thy heavenly grace,
That he may continue thine for ever,
And daily increase in thy Holy Spirit more and more,
Until he come unto thy everlasting kingdom.

* * *

*Look after me, O Lord, that I may be always with you and so become
more like you.*

O God, forasmuch as without thee we are not able to please
thee; mercifully grant that thy Holy Spirit may in all things
direct and rule our hearts; through Jesus Christ our Lord.

* * *

*O God, we cannot do your will unless you help us. Send the Holy
Spirit into our hearts to show us how to live.*

O Heavenly Father, send into our hearts and into the hearts
of everybody the spirit of our Lord Jesus Christ.

III   Breakfast-time

Each time we eat, may we remember God's love.

This prayer comes from China.

At meal times we thank God specially for his goodness. Even if you do not like what you have been given to eat, which happens sometimes, you can think, 'Oh well, some people in the world haven't got *anything* to eat this morning', and you can ask God to help them. This is a good time of day to think about homes and families and how much you love your own, and to remember all the other people who work to make the world such a lovely and exciting place to live in. Ask God to take care of them, and to help you to help them.

> Come, God, be our guest;
> May our food thus be blessed.

> *This prayer comes from Germany.*

HOME

Dear Father of the great world family, thank you for my home; for my father and mother, my sisters and brothers, relations and friends. Help us truly to love each other, and to care more for each other's good than for our own, so that we may live together as a united family in a happy home, to your honour and glory. Through Jesus Christ our Lord.

FOR PEACE

God, our Father, Creator of the world, please help us to love one another. Make nations friendly with other nations; make all of us love each other like brothers. Help us to do our part to bring peace in the world and happiness to all men.

This prayer comes from Japan.

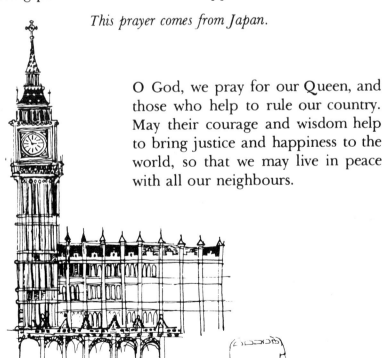

O God, we pray for our Queen, and those who help to rule our country. May their courage and wisdom help to bring justice and happiness to the world, so that we may live in peace with all our neighbours.

34

Dear God, please look after everybody at work today:
all those who drive buses and trains so that other people may go to work;
those who work in mines and quarries to get material for others to use in factories and workshops;
those who look after crops and animals on the farms to help with our food;
those who catch fish for us to eat;
those who bring our food to us, and those who sell it in shops.

Bless all those who help to look after us in any other way. Be with them in their work and help them to remember you are with us always.

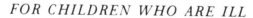

FOR CHILDREN WHO ARE ILL

Lord Jesus, who for our sakes became a man, and who showed your love of children by taking them up in your arms and blessing them: we ask you to bless those who are ill (and especially . . . .). Your love for them is greater than ours can ever be; therefore we trust them to your care and keeping.

Our Father in Heaven, thank you for the loving care of doctors and nurses who spend their lives helping sick people. We praise you for giving them clever minds and skilful hands. Guide, we pray, the teachers in colleges and hospitals where doctors and nurses are trained.

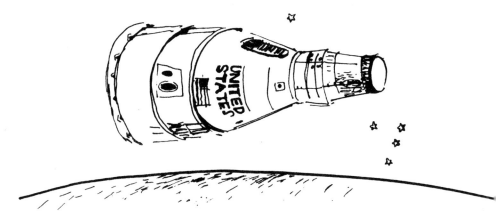

Lord of all space and distance, of all power and might, direct by your Holy Spirit the scientists and statesmen in this age of space travel and nuclear energy. Grant that their powers may be used only for your glory, to give life rather than to take it, to save nen rather than to hurt them. Banish the fear and suspicion that is poisoning the world and lead us step by step to courage and trust, for Jesus Christ's sake.

As the mighty aeroplanes fly through the air carrying their passengers and freight, be with the pilot and crew so that they will know your help and love as they carry out their task.

Then let us praise the Father, who shows us, of his grace,
The secret paths of science, the mastery of space,
The magic of the radio, the thunder of the trains,
For men made these, but God made man,
And God gave man his brains.

Father, we thank you for our animal friends: for their warm touch, their bright look, and swift movements. Help us always to treat them with kindness and care.

SOMETHING TO THINK ABOUT

For I will consider my cat Jeoffrey
For he is the servant of the living God
Daily and duly serving him.
For at the first glance of the Glory of God in the East
He worships in his way.
For this is done by wreathing his body
Seven times round with elegant quickness
For he knows that God is his Saviour
For God has bless'd him in the variety of his movements
For their is nothing sweeter than his peace when at rest.
For I am possessed of a cat surpassing in beauty,
From whom I take occasion to bless Almighty God.

Thank you, God, for my pet . . . .
By his movements may he remind me of
your goodness in creating our wonderful bodies.
By his beauty may he remind me of your
goodness in creating this wonderful
world.
By his dependence on me for his food
and shelter may he remind me of your
goodness in providing for us.
Thank you, God, for our bodies, the
world we live in and your gifts of food
and shelter.
May God, the provider of good, help
us to be providers for the helpless.

Help me, Lord, to do what I can for you. Help me to realize
that I can use every gift to your glory, and for the good of
others.

IV   Going Out and About

Forth in thy name, O Lord, I go,
My daily labour to pursue;
Thee, only thee, resolved to know,
In all I think, or speak, or do.

On the side of our church tower there is a gargoyle. Gargoyles are water spouts which usually have human or animal heads. This one is a quaint creature wearing spectacles. Perched up there he must get a very good view of everything around him! Going about your daily work or play, remember that what you are doing is part of the world's work, and pray that God will help you to get 'a very good view all round', like the gargoyle, so that you can see where you fit in. When you are out, do not forget the people who have to stay at home, particularly those who cannot go out because they are ill, and those who stay to look after them.

Go forth into the world in peace;
Be of good courage;
Hold fast that which is good;
Render to no man evil for evil;
Strengthen the faint-hearted;
Support the weak;
Help the afflicted;
Honour all men;
Love and serve the Lord,
Rejoicing in the power of the Holy Spirit.
And the blessing of God Almighty
The Father, the Son, and the Holy Ghost,*
Be upon us and remain with us for ever.

Another name for the Holy Spirit.

The Lord shall preserve thee from all evil; yea, it is even he that shall keep thy soul.

The Lord shall preserve thy going out and thy coming in, from this time forth for evermore.

* * *

God will look after us, and watch our comings and goings always.

Teach me, O God, what I ought to do: and give me faith and courage to do it, in your Name and in your strength.

Christ be with me, Christ within me,
Christ behind me, Christ before me,
Christ beside me, Christ to win me,
Christ to comfort and restore me.

Christ beneath me, Christ above me,
Christ in quiet, Christ in danger,
Christ in hearts of all that love me,
Christ in. mouth of friend and stranger.

Almighty Father, ruler of the elements and maker of the Universe in its tremendous majesty, who hast filled men with the spirit of adventure, and given them the desire to know more of thy creation; grant us the power to live and work for thee that, so forgetting self, we may do all to thy glory, and bring to our fellow men a fuller realization of the wonder of thy Presence, which is in all, and through all, and over all; through Jesus Christ our Lord.

This prayer was specially written for the men who went to explore the Antarctic in 1934.

O Lord, we beseech thee mercifully to receive the prayers of thy people which call upon thee; and grant that they may both perceive and know what things they ought to do, and also may have grace and power faithfully to fulfil the same; through Jesus Christ our Lord.

* * *

God, please listen to my prayers and let me listen to you, so that I shall know what things I ought to do, and shall be able to do them with your help.

Almighty God,
we offer thee our souls and bodies,
to be a living sacrifice,
through Jesus Christ our Lord.
Send us out into the world
in the power of thy Spirit,
to live and work
to thy praise and glory.

*　*　*

Dear God, we wish to give our whole lives to you. Send us into the world with the power of the Holy Spirit, so that our lives and works may be to your glory.

O Heavenly Father, thank you for our lovely church where we can go to worship you with all your family on earth and in heaven.

Please God, look after all those who stay behind at home when others go out to school, or work or play.

Bless the ones who are too young or too old to go, and those who look after them.

Bless those who get things ready for us when we get home, and help us to say thank you to them.

We pray especially for those who stay at home because they are ill.

Dear Father in Heaven, bless all babies, and teach us to care for them with tender love like yours, for the sake of Jesus, who was once a baby.

ROAD SAFETY

Help me, O God, as I ride my bicycle, to love my neighbour as myself, that I may do nothing to hurt or endanger any of your children. Give to my eyes clear vision, and skill to my hands and feet, and bring me safe to my journey's end, through Jesus Christ our Lord.

DISABLED CHILDREN

When I meet and work with children who are not so well and strong as I am, help me, God, to help them in the right way, so that we can all work together and take our share, for Jesus' sake.

SCHOOL

Thank you, God, for all that school means to me.
For all the things which I can find out and explore with my
mind,
               Thank you, God.
For the friends that I make,
               Thank you, God.
For all the fun of the games we play,
               Thank you, God.

      O Lord, bless our school:
      That, working together and playing together,
      We may learn to serve you, and to serve one another:
      For Jesus' sake.

Father of all men,
   We pray for boys and girls of other lands who go to our
schools. Give them courage as they live and work with those
whose words and ways are so different from their own, and
help us to be especially loving and friendly to them.

SOMETHING TO THINK ABOUT

If people do not know much, do not laugh at them, for every one of them knows something that you do not know.

This is a Gypsy proverb.

God, who has given me the power to learn, and remember, help me to look everywhere for knowledge and to love the truth and the truthful, at all times and in all places.

O all ye Works of the Lord, bless ye the Lord: praise him and
  magnify him for ever.

This is the first verse of a hymn of praise to God, which was prob-ably written about two hundred years before Jesus was born. The verses which follow are from a hymn of praise written in the twentieth century.

Great world of glory and beauty, to God lift your song!
Pay to the Father your duty, the Holy, the Strong.
When in the universe spinning you first took your place,
He was, before your beginning, the Master of Space.

All works of Man!
Give adoration
To God in whose mind
The creation began.

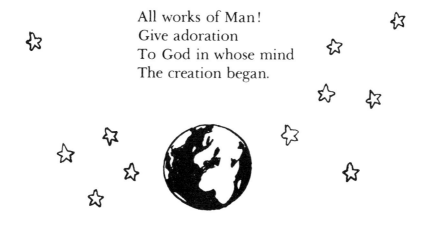

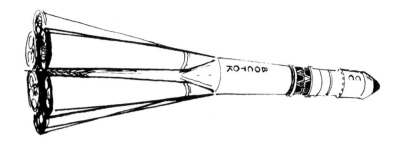

Praise him then, science revealing new truth to the mind:
Praise him, all progress in healing the ills of mankind;
Praise him, all ways of production of goods far and wide;
Praise him, all human construction, our joy and our pride.

All works of Man!
Give adoration
To God in whose mind
The creation began.

Praise him, all means of exploring the secrets of light,
Astronauts searching and soaring afar in the height,
Divers who deep in the ocean find marvels unguessed,
Seekers in mind or in motion pursuing their quest.

All works of Man!
Give adoration
To God in whose mind
The creation began.

SOMETHING TO THINK ABOUT

O good people, when you come to your journey's end,
to the low door at the sign of the World's End,
and the grim doorkeeper hands you his account,
what will you do, when you find your pockets empty?

Jesus said:

Give, and it shall be given unto you.

Help us, Lord Jesus, to give our time, money, and abilities to help those in need, whoever they are and wherever they may be. Help us to help them because they are yours, and not to consider whether they deserve it or not. Only you will know that.

A little boy once said, 'When they put Jesus in the tomb, what did they do with the other two? Didn't they bother?'

Lord help us, so that we are not the ones who pass by and leave the others.

SOMETHING TO THINK ABOUT

Long ages ago when the world was formed, the mighty mountains cooled and crumbled into rocks and small stones. Then

'In the ultimate twinkling of an eye, far tinier than the last millimetre on a six-foot rule, there came a man. He split up the one pebble which remained of all that mountain with blows; then made an arrowhead of it, and slew his brother.'

Help us, God, to use the things you have given us in the right way, so that we can help the world to become what you want it to be.

The man could have made a tool instead of a weapon, and helped his brother to till the ground, or make useful things for his comfort.

Put into the minds of scientists the thought that all inventions and ideas can be used for the good of the world, so that all people can have enough food, and cures can be found for illness and disease.

Jesus, who said 'Blessed are the Peacemakers', help us to love one another and live in peace.

V Mid-day

For every cup and plateful,
God make us truly grateful.

Just as at breakfast-time, at mid-day we specially thank God for his gifts of food and drink. When St. Francis wrote the prayer on page 54, he remembered how precious water is and thanked God for it. As you use it, think again of the people who are short of food and water, and ask God to show us how to help them. And do not forget to thank him for all the people who help *you*.

Praised be my Lord for our sister water, who is very service-
able unto us and humble and precious and clean.

This was written by St. Francis of Assisi, who lived over 750 years ago.

All good gifts around us are sent from heaven above;
Then thank the Lord, O thank the Lord for all his love.

Every time we have a meal and think of God's love, we grow
in inner strength; and as God makes me healthy in body
through the food I eat, I pray that he may give me food for
my soul.

An old Scottish Grace

Some ha'e meat, and canna eat,
    And some wad eat that want* it;
But we ha'e meat, and we can eat,
    And sae the Lord be thankit.

* *lack.*

A Jewish Grace

Blessed art thou, O Lord our God, King of the Universe, who
bringest forth food from the earth.

Holy Father, we pray for the pe ple in other lands, especially
    for the boys and girls.
Some would learn, but have no teacher;
· Some are sick, and have no doctor;
Some are sad and have no one to comfort them;
Some are hungry and poor and have no helper;
Some are happy and cared for as we are ourselves.
For all we ask your loving care.
Supply their needs and comfort their hearts, through Jesus
    Christ, our Lord.

O God, bless our hospital. Give skill to the doctors and
nurses. Comfort all who are in pain: and, if it be your will,
restore them to health. For Jesus' sake.

SOMETHING TO THINK ABOUT

The great rain is over,
The little rain begun,
Falling from the higher leaves
Bright in the sun,
Down to the lower leaves
One drop by one.

Jesus said, 'Freely ye have received; freely give.'

Help us, Lord, to be thankful for the gifts we have received
from you and to share with others who are in need.

This dirty old brown potato,
Muddy and earthy,
Dug out of the damp soil and clay—
A funny object.
A 'tater', the Cockney would call it,
I wash off the mud and there it is—
Knobbly and irregular,
Pitted with eyes—like scabs.
If I peel it or cut it
I see it is just a lump of wet starch!
Yet if I place it in the ground
Things happen;
A whole chemical factory gets to work;
The eyes sprout strange seeking white fingers,
Reaching down, down,
Sucking in nourishment through tiny hairs;
One or two shoot up, split, spread, get pink
Then green, into light,
Grow leaves, become a plant
Flowering in sunlight.
The soppy lump of starch gets slimy and black,
Dying in its own life—
Come tubers, lots of little potatoes,
Swell, grow,
Provide food and wealth!
What a miracle, Lord,
In this dirty old brown potato!

VI   Going Out and About Again

Praise the Lord, O my soul, and all that is within me praise
    his holy Name.
Praise the Lord, O my soul, and forget not all his benefits.

As you begin your afternoon, remember the weather-vane and the gargoyle. Point the right way and take a good look all round.

Perhaps you are going out for the afternoon, or perhaps it is games at school. In any case, share your good time and be happy. There is an old saying that a joy shared is a joy doubled and a sorrow shared is a sorrow halved. Work that out and prove it for yourself.

SOMETHING TO THINK ABOUT

O you shoulders, elbows, wrists,
  bless him, praise him, magnify him for ever;
you fittings of thumbs and fingers,
  bless ye the Lord;
hips, thighs, spine in its multiples,
  bless him, praise him, magnify him for ever.

Thank you, God, for the games and sport I take part in.
Thank you for movement, and for the wonderful way my
    body is put together, and works.
God, who made me, give me work to do for you.

> For the highways and lanes,
> We praise you, God.
> For the bread we eat,
> We praise you, God.
> For the lark and the wheat fields,
> We praise you, God.
> For the joy of friendship,
> We praise you, God.
>
> O father of goodness,
> We thank you each one
> For happiness, healthiness,
> Friendship and fun,
> For good things we think of,
> And good things we do,
> And all that is beautiful,
> Loving and true.

This prayer comes from France.

O God our Father, please help blind people to enjoy the sounds they hear and deaf people to enjoy the lovely things they see. We ask it in Jesus' Name.

O Lord, open my eyes, to see what is beautiful:
My mind, to know what is true,
My heart, to love what is good:
For Jesus' sake.

I come in the little things,
Saith the Lord:
Not borne on the morning's wings
Of majesty, but I have set my feet
Amidst the delicate and bladed wheat.

I come in the little things,
Saith the Lord:
Yea! on the glancing wing
Of eager birds, the softly pattering feet
Of furred and gentle beasts.

I come in the little things,
Saith the Lord.

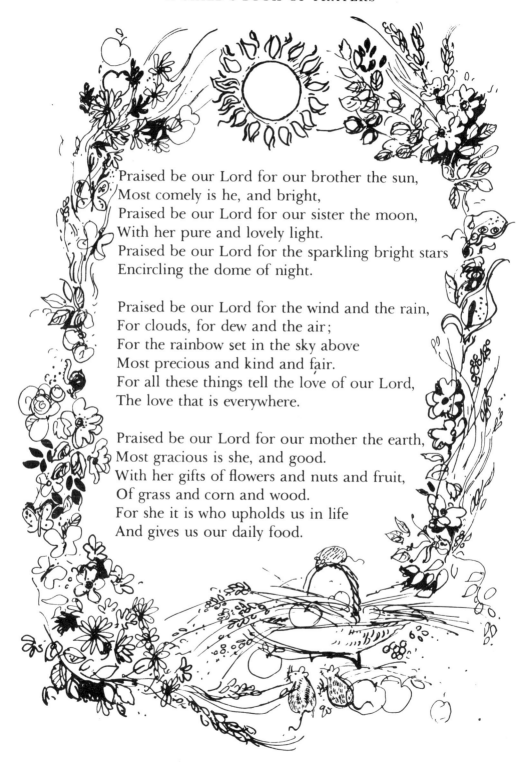

Praised be our Lord for our brother the sun,
Most comely is he, and bright,
Praised be our Lord for our sister the moon,
With her pure and lovely light.
Praised be our Lord for the sparkling bright stars
Encircling the dome of night.

Praised be our Lord for the wind and the rain,
For clouds, for dew and the air;
For the rainbow set in the sky above
Most precious and kind and fair.
For all these things tell the love of our Lord,
The love that is everywhere.

Praised be our Lord for our mother the earth,
Most gracious is she, and good.
With her gifts of flowers and nuts and fruit,
Of grass and corn and wood.
For she it is who upholds us in life
And gives us our daily food.

Our Father, maker of this wonderful world, thank you for
    Saturday, for holiday time and freedom and the open air.
Come into all I am going to do today at home, out of doors,
    with my friends.
Help me to enjoy everything you have made for me.
For Jesus' sake.

Lord Jesus, be with those who have no happy holidays, who
have never seen the sea or played in the fields. If there is
something that we can do to make them happier, please show
us, and if there is something that we can share, help us to do
it gladly for your sake.

SOMETHING TO THINK ABOUT

For wherever a saint has dwelt, wherever a martyr has given
    his blood for the blood of Christ,
There is holy ground, and the sanctity shall not depart from
    it,
Though armies trample over it, though sightseers come with
    guide books looking over it.

Jesus, who gave your life for us, once for all, help us to re-
    member your followers who gave their lives for the things
    they believed in.
Help us to think of the great cathedrals they knew as places
    where they worshipped and loved you; their little homes
    and houses as places where they loved their families, and
    did your will; the open spaces where they lived, worked
    and worshipped as places where we can do the same.
Help us all to find you in the places where they found you.

God said:

In every place where you find the imprint of men's feet, there am I.

This is from a Jewish holy book.

Help us to remember God is everywhere.

God is in thy heart, yet thou searchest for him in the wilderness.

This is from a Sikh holy book.

VII Coming Home: Spending the Evening

We thank you, Loving Father,
For all your tender care,
For food and clothes and shelter
And all the world so fair.

Home! We take it for granted that there is a welcome there for us. Make sure that other people can take it for granted that you will be thankful for all they do for you. Some people have no homes; some people have no family to welcome them. Don't forget them, but when you thank God for your own home ask him to take care of them.

SOMETHING TO THINK ABOUT

. . . And the garden gate stands open and the house door
    swings before us,
And the candles twinkle happily as we lie down.

For here the noble lady is who greets us from our wandering,
Here are all the sensible and very needful things,
Here are blankets, here is milk, here are rest and slumber,
And the courteous prince of angels with the fire about his
    wings.

Lord of the loving heart,
May mine be loving too.
Lord of the gentle hands,
May mine be gentle too.
Lord of the willing feet,
May mine be willing too.
So may I grow more like to thee
In all I say and do.

O Loving Father of all your children,
We thank you for all your blessings, day by day.
For home and friends and all who show us kindness.
For health and strength, for sight and hearing,
For fresh air and sunshine,
For all the beauty of your world,
For games and toys and laughter,
For art and books and music.
For all that gladdens and blesses our life.

Love and praise to you we give
By whose love all creatures live.

FOR REFUGEES AND THE HOMELESS

Oh, to have a little house!
　To own the hearth and stool and all!
The heaped-up sods upon the fire,
　The pile of turf against the wall!

To have a clock with weights and chains
　And pendulum swinging up and down,
A dresser filled with shining delph,*
　Speckled and white and blue and brown!

I could be busy all the day
　Clearing and sweeping hearth and floor,
And fixing on their shelf again
　My white and blue and speckled store!

I could be quiet there at night
　Beside the fire and by myself,
Sure of a bed, and loth to leave
　The ticking clock and the shining delph!

This means pottery.

Och! but I'm weary of mist and dark,
  And roads where there's never a house or bush,
And tired I am of bog and road
  And the crying wind and the lonesome hush!

And I am praying to God on high,
  And I am praying him night and day,
For a little house, a house of my own—
  Out of the wind's and the rain's way.

The Old Woman wanted to be busy all the day.
  We pray for those who have no work, and those who for
any reason cannot do the work they would like.

She wanted to be quiet at night and sure of a bed.
  We pray for those who cannot sleep, and those who have
no shelter. Help them, Lord.

Dear Jesus, who was taken as a baby refugee into Egypt,
take care of all homeless wanderers,
  of all who have to leave their comfortable homes
because of misfortune or war,
  and of all who have no homes at all.
Guide them with your love to find help and friends, and to
    help each other in their loneliness.

We thank you, Father, for our minds to think and our hands to work, and for all the fun of making things ourselves. Help us to use what we can do to help others, and to do it well so that you may look at our work and be glad.

Thank you, God, for the gift of music. May I not neglect it, but use its power and beauty to lead me nearer to yourself. Whether I sing or play or listen, and whether the music is a hymn or a song or a symphony, may I be blessed through this gift of yours, and cherish it always.

I do not ask, O Lord, that you will think my thoughts for me or do my work for me, but that you will help me; so that what is too hard for me to do alone, and what is too difficult for me to understand by myself, I may be able to do and understand because you are with me. Teach me to think of Jesus as my friend and as one who is always by my side, for his Name's sake.

O God, our Heavenly Father, thank you for the Bible, which tells us so much about you, and about those who have helped and served you in days gone by, and especially for the great story of Jesus and how he came to be our Leader. Give us strength and courage to be his true followers.

God be in my head, and in my understanding;
God be in my eyes, and in my looking;
God be in my mouth, and in my speaking ;
God be in my heart, and in my thinking;
God be at my end, and at my departing.

A PRAYER FOR WHEN YOU ARE UNHAPPY

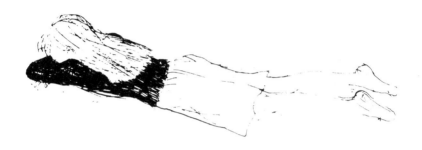

When sad and dreadful things happen to me, help me, Lord,
to remember that you died for me, rose again and said:

'I am with you always.'

Then I know my strength will be enough for what I have to
bear.

When my work seems very hard I can say:

For work to do and strength to do the work,
We thank you, Lord.

The Lord is my strength, and my shield; my heart hath trusted
in him, and I am helped: therefore my heart danceth for joy,
and in my song will I praise him.

73

O praise God in his holiness, praise him in the firmament of
his power.

Praise him in his noble acts, praise him according to his
excellent greatness.

Praise him in the sound of the trumpet, praise him upon the
lute and harp.

Praise him in the cymbals and dances, praise him upon the
strings and pipe.

Praise him upon the well-tuned cymbals, praise him upon the
loud cymbals.

Let every thing that hath breath praise the Lord.

Holy, holy, holy, Lord God of hosts, heaven and earth are
full of thy glory: glory be to thee, O Lord most High.

VIII   Bedtime

Glory be to thee, Lord Jesus, for all my happy days.

A Monkey and a Mandarin,
A Mistress and a Mouse,
Were teasing a Tall Tangerine
Because he had no house.
'It seems a shameful thing,' they said,
'To have no place to go to bed.'

This is a little rhyme that, although it is nonsense, can teach us all a great deal. It *is* a shameful thing that there are people without a place to go to bed. The Tangerine did not need one really, but lots of people do, and of course teasing will not help. What will?

When I pray I speak to God,
When I listen God speaks to me.
I am now in his Presence. He is very near to me.

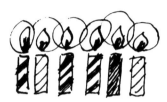

O Lord Jesus, light a candle in our hearts, that we may see
what is therein and so make clean thy dwelling place.

This prayer comes from Africa.

Forgive me, Lord, for thy dear Son,
The ill that I this day have done,
That with the world, myself, and thee,
I, ere I sleep, at peace may be.

Our Father in Heaven:
Please forgive me for the things I have done wrong:
For bad temper and angry words;
For being greedy and wanting the best for myself;
For making other people unhappy:
Forgive me, Heavenly Father.

May God, my Heavenly Father, who has forgiven me so many
times, make me forgiving too.

Almighty God, our Heavenly Father,
we have sinned against thee,
through our own fault,
in thought, and word, and deed,
and in what we have left undone.

For thy Son·our Lord Jesus Christ's sake,
forgive us all that is past;
and grant that we may serve thee
in newness of life,
to the glory of thy Name.

O give thanks unto the Lord, for he is gracious, and his mercy endureth for ever.

O Lord Jesus Christ, who received the children who came to you, receive also from me, your child, this evening prayer. Shelter me under the shadow of your wings, that in peace I may lie down and sleep; and waken me in due time, that I may glorify you, for you alone are righteous and merciful.

This prayer is used by the Eastern Church.

Lord Jesus,
Thank you for being born for us,
Thank you for living for us,
Thank you for bearing things we have to bear,
Thank you for telling us about the Father,
Thank you for dying for us,
Thank you for rising again for us
Thank you for being with us always.

O God, who hast prepared for them that love thee such good things as pass man's understanding: pour into our hearts such love toward thee, that we, loving thee above all things, may obtain thy promises, which exceed all that we can desire; through Jesus Christ our Lord.

* * *

O God, who will make us more happy than we can imagine, make us fit to receive your gifts and love you always.

A PRAYER FOR EVERYBODY IN THE HOUSE

Save us, O Lord, while waking, and guard us while sleeping, that awake we may watch with Christ, and asleep we may rest in peace.

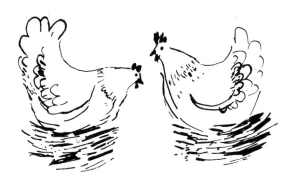

Jesus Christ, thou Child so wise,
Bless my hands and fill my eyes
And bring my soul to Paradise.

IX   Night

May God, our Heavenly Father, bless and keep his children, this night and for ever.

Night-time for you; the beginning of a new day for people in some other parts of the world who are now waking up to

THINK AND THANK GOD OF ALL

Glory to thee, my God, this night,
For all the blessings of the light;
Keep me, O keep me, King of kings,
Beneath thy own almighty wings.

Lord Jesus,
Thank you for taking care of me today;
Help me to love you more and more
    Every day of my life.

Jesus Divine, dear Brother mine,
Be with me all the day.
And when the light has turned to night
Be with me still, I pray.
Where'er I be, come thou with me
And never go away.

For your goodness at all times, and your presence in all
    places,
    Glory be to thee, O God.
For the memory of things past, for the use of things present
    and for the hope of things to come,
    Glory be to thee, O God.

Loving Father, hear our prayer
    For thy children everywhere;
However different they may be,
    All girls and boys belong to thee;
And those who live so far away
    Are just as much thy family.
Loving Father, hear our prayer
    For thy children everywhere.

Let us remember the whole family of God,
    the children of Africa, of Europe and of the East,
    the children of the Commonwealth,
    the children of America and Russia,
    of the islands and the mountains and lands of snow.
They all have lovely gifts to bring to God.
We need their help and friendship.
God, please help them and bless them today and help us to
    live
so that they can trust us.
May we learn together how to serve you on earth as it is in
    Heaven.
                    For Jesus' sake.

SOMETHING TO THINK ABOUT

Then as Now; and Now as Then,
Spins on this World of Men,
White—Black—Yellow—Red:
They wake, work, eat, play, go to bed.
Black—Yellow—Red—White:
They talk, laugh, weep, dance, morn to night.
Yellow—Red—White—Black:
Sun shine, moon rides, clouds come back.

As o'er each continent and island
　　The dawn leads on another day,
The voice of prayer is never silent,
　　Nor dies the strain of praise away.

The sun that bids us rest is waking
　　Our brethren 'neath the western sky,
And hour by hour fresh lips are making
　　Thy wondrous doings heard on high.

Bless, O Lord, we pray you, those who wake and work that we may sleep; the policeman and the fireman who protect us; those who look after people who are ill; those who work beneath the earth; those who serve our commerce by road, rail, sea and air, and those who carry our news to near or distant places.

Guard them as they guard and serve us, and watch over them in danger and loneliness, for the sake of him who prayed for us in the watches of the night, Jesus Christ, our Lord.

O Heavenly Father, protect and bless all things that have breath: guard them from all evil and let them sleep in peace.

Praise God, from whom all blessings flow,
Praise him, all creatures here below,
Praise him above, ye heavenly host,
Praise Father, Son, and Holy Ghost.*

* *Another name for the Holy Spirit.*

SOMETHING TO THINK ABOUT

Light looked down and beheld Darkness.
　'Thither will I go,' said Light.
Peace looked down and beheld War.
　'Thither will I go,' said Peace.
Love looked down and beheld Hatred.
　'Thither will I go,' said Love.
So came Light and shone.
So came Peace and gave rest.
So came Love and brought Life.
And the Word* was made Flesh, and dwelt among us.

　* *This is the way St. John describes the birth of Jesus.*

The peace of God, which passeth all understanding, keep our hearts and minds in the knowledge and love of God, and of his Son Jesus Christ our Lord.

The grace of our Lord Jesus Christ, and the love of God, and the fellowship of the Holy Spirit, be with us all evermore.

Glory be to the Father, and to the Son: and to the Holy
    Ghost;
As it was in the beginning, is now, and ever shall be: world
    without end.

Subject Index

Sometimes you will have to look through a whole prayer (if it is a long one), or the whole of one of the passages called 'Something to think about', in order to find the subject which you have looked up in this index. For example, under the heading 'Earth' is a reference to the passage 'The God who created the heavens' on page 16. When you turn to that page, you will find that the reference to earth is in the sixth line of the passage.

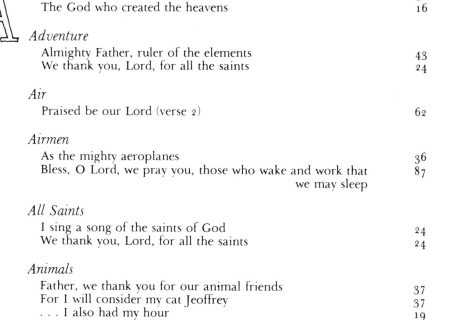

SUBJECT INDEX

SUBJECT INDEX

94

SUBJECT INDEX

SUBJECT INDEX

97

SUBJECT INDEX

SUBJECT INDEX

SUBJECT INDEX

SUBJECT INDEX

School   *Page*
    Father of all men, we pray for boys and girls of other lands   46
    If people do not know much   47
    O Lord, bless our school   46
    Thank you, God, for all that school means   46

Science
    O all ye works of the Lord   47
    Then let us praise the Father   36

Scientists
    Long ages ago when the world was formed   50
    Lord of all space and distance   36

Sea, The,   see also *Sailors and Fishermen*
    O all ye works of the Lord   47

Seasons, The
    Praise the Lord for all the seasons   13
    Spring For flowers that bloom about our feet   14
    Summer We thank you, O loving Father, for the joys that   14
            summer brings
    Autumn I praise you, God, for all the joys of autumn   15
    Winter Heavenly Father, thank you for the joys of winter   15
            O God, my Father in Heaven, thank you for clear   15
                frosty days

Self
    {Almighty God, we offer thee our souls and bodies
    {Dear God, we wish to give our whole lives   }44
    Grant, O Heavenly Father, that I may be glad through all   28
                this day
    Jesus Christ, thou Child so wise   80
    Jesus may I be like you   29
    Long ages ago when the world was formed   50
    May my mouth praise the love of God this morning   29
    {O Lord, we beseech thee mercifully to receive the prayers
    {God, please listen   }43

Service,   see also *Helping Other People*
    Almighty God, our Heavenly Father, we have sinned   79
    Let us remember the whole family of God   85
    O Lord, bless our school   46

Shelter
    For I will consider my cat Jeoffrey   37
    Heavenly Father, thank you for the joys of winter   15
    Oh, to have a little house!   70
    We thank you, loving Father   65

SUBJECT INDEX

SUBJECT INDEX

SUBJECT INDEX

SUBJECT INDEX